Before his first plane trip Grandpa Simple was told chewing gum would keep his ears from popping during the flight.

After the plane landed, Grandma Simple asked, "Did the gum help, dear?"

"Yep, worked fine," replied Grandpa Simple. "Only trouble is I can't get the gum out of my ears."

THE FIRST SIMPLE FAMILY JOKE BOOK

Adam Bryan

BALLANTINE BOOKS • NEW YORK

Copyright © 1991 by Thomas S. Roberts

All rights reserved under International and Pan-American Copyright Conventions. Published in the United States of America by Ballantine Books, a division of Random House, Inc., New York, and simultaneously in Canada by Random House of Canada Limited, Toronto.

Library of Congress Catalog Card Number: 91-91970

ISBN 0-345-37234-4

Manufactured in the United States of America

First Edition: September 1991

Why did Willie Simple tiptoe past the medicine cabinet?

Because he didn't want to wake up the sleeping pills.

Why did Susie Simple throw her alarm clock out the window?

She wanted to see time fly.

Why did Mrs. Simple drive her car off a cliff?

She wanted to test her new air brakes.

Why did Uncle Maynard Simple, the great trapeze artist, refuse to fly?

The airline wouldn't put a net under the plane.

Mr. Simple hit a woman with his car and knocked her twenty feet in the air. Why did he sue her?

For leaving the scene of the accident.

Why did Grandpa Simple move out of his house?

Because he heard most accidents happen at home.

Why did Grandpa Simple cut a hole in the rug?
He wanted to see a floor show.

How did Grandma Simple get to the hospital?
By accident.

Why did Great Aunt Irma Simple run over the same man twice?
There wasn't anyone else on the street.

What did Willie Simple say when the teacher asked him why he was standing on one leg?

"I'll fall down if I lift the other leg, too."

Why did Grandpa Simple run a steam roller over his potato field?

He wanted to raise mashed potatoes.

What did Susie Simple say when the teacher said, "Your story about the cat is exactly the same as the one your brother Willie wrote."

"It's the same cat."

Mr. Simple looked up from his newspaper and said, "There's a story here that says there's a man run over on New York City streets every eight minutes."

"That's awful," replied Mrs. Simple. "Someone should tell him to stay on the sidewalk."

Grandpa Simple went to Doctor Sigmund Simple and complained that his left knee hurt.

"That's just old age," said Doctor Simple.

"The other one's just as old," replied Grandpa Simple, "so why doesn't it hurt, too?"

MRS. SIMPLE: Wake up.

MR. SIMPLE: Why? Go back to sleep.

MRS. SIMPLE: I heard a mouse squeak.

MR. SIMPLE: What do you want me to do, oil it?

Willie Simple asked his mother: "Would you spank me for something I didn't do?"

"Certainly not," replied Mrs. Simple. "Why do you ask?"

"I didn't do my homework."

At a family picnic Grandpa Simple said, "When I was twelve, I ran off with the circus."

"Gee," said Susie Simple, "was it fun?"

"I don't know," replied Grandpa Simple. "The police made me bring it back."

WILLIE SIMPLE: Do you have holes in your underwear?

COUSIN CINDY SIMPLE: What a disgusting question! Of course I don't.

WILLIE SIMPLE: How do you get your legs in, then?

"I'm losing my memory," Grandma Simple told Grandpa Simple, "and I'm worried about it."

"Nonsense," replied Grandpa Simple. "Just forget about it."

How many Simples does it take to change a light bulb?

Five. One to hold the light bulb and four to turn the ladder.

What did Willie Simple say when Mrs. Simple asked him how he did on his first day of school?

"Not so good. Teacher says I have to go back tomorrow."

UNCLE MAYNARD SIMPLE: Is your water good for
  drinking?
FARMER JAKE SIMPLE: Sure is. It's well water.

Mr. Simple and Cousin Elmer Simple had been
hunting for hours when Mr. Simple complained,
"We've been out here all day and haven't shot
anything."

"I know," said Cousin Elmer. "Maybe we
should bring our guns next time."

Aunt Edna Simple went to the post office to
mail a package, and the clerk said, "This is too
heavy. You'll have to put more stamps on it."

Aunt Edna scratched her head and said, "But
won't that make it even heavier?"

WILLIE SIMPLE: This coffee is terrible.

WAITRESS: Young man, I've been making coffee since before you were born.

WILLIE SIMPLE: Well, I sure wish you hadn't saved it for me.

"I just dreamed you bought me a beautiful new sports car and a new mink coat," said Mrs. Simple.

Mr. Simple groaned and said, "Why don't you go back to sleep and enjoy them?"

Mr. Simple was seriously injured in an automobile accident and was taken to a hospital where he lay unconscious for quite a while. Later the doctor came into the room with Mrs. Simple and said, "I'm afraid your husband is dead."

At just that moment Mr. Simple woke up and said, "No I'm not."

"Shut up!" said Mrs. Simple. "Do you think you know more than the doctor does?"

9

GRANDPA SIMPLE: I just swallowed a chicken bone.

GRANDMA SIMPLE: Are you choking?

GRANDPA SIMPLE: Of course not. I'm serious.

Mrs. Simple went to the grocery store and complained to the manager that the flour she had bought the day before was too tough.

"Too tough!" replied the astonished grocer.

"That's right," said Mrs. Simple. "I made cookies with it, and no one in my family could chew them."

Before his first plane trip, Grandpa Simple was told chewing gum would keep his ears from popping during the flight.

After the plane landed, Grandma Simple asked, "Did the gum help, dear?"

"Yep, worked fine," replied Grandpa Simple. "Only trouble is, I can't get the gum out of my ears."

What did Susie Simple say when her mother told her it took three sheep to make a wool sweater?

"Wow! I didn't even know they could knit."

When Willie Simple told his mother he had knocked over the ladder by the side of the house, she said, "You'd better go tell your father."

"Oh, he knows," replied Willie. "He was on it."

A pilot who took Grandpa and Grandma Simple for their first ride in an airplane with an open cockpit decided to have a little fun. He told them he wouldn't charge them if neither made a sound when he did a loop-the-loop and a sudden nose dive. They agreed, and the pilot performed the stunts.

As the plane came in for a landing, the pilot yelled back to Grandma and Grandpa Simple: "How'd you like it?"

"Great," replied Grandpa, "but I almost let out a yell when Grandma fell out."

Cousin Elmer Simple got fired from his job as a street sweeper because he couldn't keep his mind in the gutter.

When Mr. and Mrs. Simple went to the theater, the ticket seller asked, "Do you want ten-dollar seats downstairs or five-dollar seats upstairs?"

"Gee," said Mr. Simple, "what's playing upstairs?"

Cousin Elmer Simple was so stupid that he had to take off his mittens to count up to ten.

What did Mr. Simple say when the judge told him, "I'm going to give you thirty days or thirty dollars"?

"I'll take the thirty dollars."

Grandpa Simple complained that Grandma Simple gossiped so much that her tongue got sunburned whenever she went to the beach.

Why did Cousin Elmer Simple cross a potato with a sponge?

So it would soak up more gravy.

Why did Mr. Simple get rid of his bird dog?
Because it couldn't fly.

Mr. Simple rushed home and exclaimed,
"Guess what, dear? We don't have to move into
a more expensive apartment. The landlord just
raised the rent on this one."

GAS STATION OWNER: Didn't you apply for a job
  here last week?
WILLIE SIMPLE: Yes, sir, I did.
GAS STATION OWNER: I thought I told you I
  needed an older boy.
WILLIE SIMPLE: That's why I came back.

Willie Simple came home with a skunk one day, and Mrs. Simple said, "What are you going to do with that skunk?"

"Keep him as a pet," replied Willie.

"But what about the smell?"

"Don't worry," said Willie. "He won't mind."

MRS. SIMPLE: Willie, go outside and water the garden.

WILLIE SIMPLE: But, Mom, it's raining.

MRS. SIMPLE: So, put your raincoat on.

Cousin Elmer Simple went to a factory for a job interview. The boss looked over his application and said, "You're asking for a lot of money considering you don't have any experience."

"The way I see it," replied Cousin Elmer, "is it's harder to do the work when you don't have experience."

15

Then there was the time when Great Uncle Abner Simple went down to the marriage bureau to see if his license had expired.

Great Aunt Sally Simple was so fat that every time she fell down she rocked herself to sleep trying to get up.

DRIVER'S LICENSE EXAMINER: Have your eyes ever been checked?
GRANDPA SIMPLE: Of course not! They've always been brown.

MR. SIMPLE: How many bushels of apples do you expect to get from that tree?
FARMER JAKE SIMPLE: None.
MR. SIMPLE: None! How come?
FARMER JAKE SIMPLE: It's a peach tree.

GRANDPA SIMPLE: You know I don't like this Swiss cheese with holes in it.
GRANDMA SIMPLE: I know, dear. Just eat the cheese, and leave the holes on the plate.

Mr. Simple and Cousin Elmer Simple went to a car lot to buy a used car. But they didn't have enough money, so the salesman sold them a donkey.

"Does this donkey stop at red lights?" asked Cousin Elmer Simple.

"Certainly," said the salesman. "It stops at red lights and goes on green."

Mr. Simple and Cousin Elmer Simple left on the back of the donkey, but in fifteen minutes they were back at the car lot without the animal.

"Where's the donkey?" asked the salesman.

"Well," replied Mr. Simple, "we stopped at a red light, and a car pulled up beside us. Then someone yelled, 'Look at those two idiots on the donkey!' We got off to see who the two idiots were, and the donkey ran away."

17

Why did Grandpa Simple have all his teeth pulled?

So he'd have more gum to chew.

AUNT EDNA SIMPLE: Why don't you peel the banana before you eat it?
GREAT UNCLE ABNER SIMPLE: Why should I? I know what's inside.

What's the first thing Uncle Maynard Simple does when he gets out of the shower?

He takes all his clothes off.

MR. SIMPLE: Willie, you be good while your mother and I are gone.

WILLIE SIMPLE: I'll be good for a dollar.

MR. SIMPLE: When I was a boy, I was good for nothing.

Why did Grandpa Simple wear only one boot when he went into town?

Because he heard there was a 50 percent chance of snow.

When Grandma Simple heard postal rates were going to be raised to 29 cents, she went to the post office and bought all the 25-cent stamps they had.

Why couldn't Mrs. Simple fill the salt shaker?
Because she couldn't get the salt through the little holes.

Willie Simple and Cousin Elmer Simple were walking through a field on Farmer Jake Simple's farm one night when they came to a high fence.

"How are we going to get over it?" asked Cousin Elmer.

"Easy," said Willie Simple. "I'll just shine my flashlight up over it, and you climb up the beam."

"Ha! I know better than that!" said Cousin Elmer. "Soon as I get halfway up, you'll turn the light off."

Why did Willie Simple fill his sneakers with birdseed?
To feed his pigeon toes.

Aunt Edna Simple was so skinny she wore suspenders to hold up her girdle.

Why did Willie Simple put a blindfold on?
So he could go on a blind date.

Why did Mr. and Mrs. Simple hire a tutor for Susie Simple?
So she could pass recess.

TEACHER: Susie, what's the difference between your age and Willie's?

SUSIE SIMPLE: Let's see. Last year my mother said Willie was one year older than me. But that was a year ago, so now we must be the same age.

GRANDPA SIMPLE: Susie, how much is two plus two?

SUSIE SIMPLE: Three.

GRANDPA SIMPLE: What a smart girl you are. You only missed it by two.

GREAT UNCLE ABNER SIMPLE: I've been seeing spots before my eyes.

AUNT EDNA SIMPLE: Have you seen the doctor?

GREAT UNCLE ABNER SIMPLE: Nope, just spots.

TEACHER: Willie, what does heredity mean?

WILLIE SIMPLE: It means that if your mom and dad didn't have any kids, you probably won't either.

TEACHER: Susie, spell mouse.

SUSIE SIMPLE: M-o-u-s.

TEACHER: What's at the end of it?

SUSIE SIMPLE: A tail.

One day Grandpa Simple took Susie Simple to the zoo. They stopped at the giraffe pen, and Grandpa asked, "Do you know why we call this animal a giraffe?"

Susie Simple thought for a moment and then said, "Because it has a real long neck."

"But," said Grandpa Simple, "why would its long neck make us call it a giraffe?"

"That's easy," replied Susie Simple. "Did you ever see a giraffe with a short neck?"

TEACHER: How do you spell Mississippi?
WILLIE SIMPLE: The state or the river?

What has an I.Q. of 120?
   The entire Simple family.

When Willie Simple got a new watch, Susie Simple asked, "Does it tell time?"
   "No," answered Willie. "I have to look at it."

Cousin Elmer Simple once called the camera store to see if he could rent some flash bulbs.

Willie Simple got a job as a carpenter and was working on the side of a house. He looked at a nail and threw it on the ground. He threw the next nail away, too. And the next, and the next.

"Why are you throwing all those nails away?" asked Cousin Elmer Simple, who had been watching him.

"They're no good," said Willie. "The heads are on the wrong side."

"You're an idiot!" shouted Cousin Elmer. "They're for the other side of the house."

GRANDPA SIMPLE: Sometimes one person's illness is another person's blessing.

DOCTOR SIGMUND SIMPLE: What do you mean by that?

GRANDPA SIMPLE: Grandma Simple got laryngitis a few days ago, and my ears haven't bothered me since.

Uncle Maynard Simple walked into Doctor Sigmund Simple's office. His clothes were torn, and he was bleeding everywhere.

"Have an accident?" asked Doctor Sigmund Simple.

"No thanks," replied Uncle Maynard Simple. "I already had one."

CUSTOMER: Give me two hotdogs, one with ketchup, one without.
SUSIE SIMPLE: Which one?

Great Aunt Irma Simple has a collection of antique jewelry. She bought it when it was new.

26

MRS. SIMPLE: Your face is clean, but how did your hands get so dirty?
WILLIE SIMPLE: Washing my face.

SUSIE SIMPLE: Grandpa, do you think flies are happy?
GRANDPA SIMPLE: Have you ever heard one complain?

Why did the Simples always take their vacation to the seashore in December?
To avoid the crowds.

It was so cold when the Simples went to the beach that they used antifreeze instead of suntan lotion.

Willie Simple was late on his first day as a salesman on the second floor of a men's clothing store.

When his new boss asked why he was late, he said, "The escalator broke down, and I was stuck on it for over an hour."

TEACHER: What is a caterpillar after it's one week old?
SUSIE SIMPLE: Two weeks old.

MRS. SIMPLE: Did you turn off your light?
SUSIE SIMPLE: I couldn't find the switch. It's too dark in here.

What did Mrs. Simple do when the mechanic said her car needed a new muffler?
She knitted one.

What did Grandma Simple do when she received a letter from Willie Simple saying he had grown another foot since she had last seen him?
She knitted another sock.

Why doesn't anyone ever call Cousin Elmer Simple a quitter?

He's been fired from every job he's ever had.

SUNDAY SCHOOL TEACHER: Who was the luckiest man in the Bible?
WILLIE SIMPLE: Adam.
SUNDAY SCHOOL TEACHER: Why?
WILLIE SIMPLE: Because he didn't have a mother-in-law.

TEACHER: Where do we find elephants?
SUSIE SIMPLE: We don't have to find them. They're so big they never get lost.

MRS. SIMPLE: Did you hear what Cindy Simple's friends did before her wedding?

MR. SIMPLE: No, what?

MRS. SIMPLE: Instead of giving her a shower, they made her take one.

GREAT AUNT SALLY SIMPLE: Do you serve crabs in this restaurant?

WAITER: Sit down, madam. We serve anyone here.

Aunt Edna Simple and Cousin Elmer Simple went to the beach for their vacation. While Cousin Elmer was swimming, a shark bit off one of his toes. He swam to shore as fast as he could and yelled to Aunt Edna, telling her what had happened.

Aunt Edna rushed toward him and gasped, "Which one was it?"

"How would I know?" said Cousin Elmer. "All sharks look the same to me."

GRANDPA SIMPLE: I have a ringing in my ears. What shall I do about it?
DOCTOR SIGMUND SIMPLE: Don't answer it.

Shortly after Uncle Archibald Simple and Aunt Agatha Simple were married, they both came down with what seemed to be the same illness. After several days of suffering, they realized they needed a doctor's help. But Uncle Archibald was so cheap that he decided to send only Aunt Agatha to the doctor, figuring he could follow the same advice the doctor gave her.

After Aunt Agatha got home from the doctor's office, Uncle Archibald asked what was wrong with them. "Well," said Aunt Agatha, "I don't like having to tell you this, but we're pregnant."

GRANDMA SIMPLE: When Cousin Martha Simple was young, she could have married anyone she pleased.
GRANDPA SIMPLE: Then why didn't she ever marry?
GRANDMA SIMPLE: She never pleased anyone.

LAWYER: Why do you want a divorce?

COUSIN IDA SIMPLE: My husband brings his work home every night.

LAWYER: What's wrong with that?

COUSIN IDA SIMPLE: He's a garbage man.

Susie and Willie Simple, on a bicycle built for two, had a hard time getting up a steep hill.

When they finally got to the top, Willie said, "Whew! I didn't think we'd ever make it."

"Me, too," exclaimed Susie. "It's a good thing I kept the brakes on, or we'd have rolled back down."

How did Cousin Elmer Simple pass his I.Q. test?

He cheated.

Willie Simple walked out onto a pier and fell into the ocean. Fortunately, Grandpa Simple happened to be passing by, and he saw what had happened.

After Grandpa Simple had pulled Willie from the water, he asked, "How'd you come to fall in?"

"I didn't come to fall in!" replied Willie. "I came to fish."

GREAT UNCLE ABNER SIMPLE: Yep, my dog got loose the other day and bit the postman, so I had to shoot him.

COUSIN ELMER SIMPLE: Your dog was mad, huh?

GREAT UNCLE ABNER SIMPLE: Well, he wasn't too happy about it.

Willie Simple rushed into the house yelling, "Dad, someone's stealing your car."

Mr. Simple ran outside, but returned right away.

"Did you stop him?" Willie asked.

"No," replied Mr. Simple. "He was going too fast. But I got his license number."

Aunt Edna Simple was walking down the street with a scrawny, miserable looking chicken under her arm.

Mr. Simple saw her and said, "Where'd you get it?

"I won her in a raffle," said the chicken.

UNCLE MAYNARD SIMPLE: We had been hunting in the jungle for only a few minutes when I spotted a leopard.

COUSIN ELMER SIMPLE: Aw, don't try to fool me; they come that way.

Uncle Maynard Simple went to the bank to cash a check. Since he didn't have an account there, the teller asked if he could identify himself.

Uncle Maynard went to the bank window and stared at his reflection for a moment. He then went back to the teller and said, "Yep, it's me, all right."

35

Mr. and Mrs. Simple were very worried about their daughter, Susie, because she never spoke. In fact, at age seven, she hadn't ever said a single word. Then one night at the supper table Susie suddenly said, "Please pass the ketchup."

After getting over her shock, Mrs. Simple said, "How come you haven't talked until now?"

"Well," replied Susie, "up until now everything was all right."

Susie Simple loves going to the doctor so she can stick her tongue out at him.

Mr. Simple went to the library to borrow a book, but he came back home empty-handed.

"I thought you were going to check out a book," said Mrs. Simple.

"I was," replied Mr. Simple, "but when I got to the library, there was a sign on the door that said: 'LIBRARY CLOSED. BOOK WAS STOLEN.' "

Why was Cousin Elmer Simple's application to become an astronaut turned down?

NASA said there wasn't enough space for him.

JUDGE: Why did you park your car there?
MRS. SIMPLE: There was a sign that said: FINE FOR PARKING.

Willie Simple took his date to the theater and asked the ticket seller for two tickets.

"Sorry," said the woman in the booth, "we have standing room only."

"Oh," replied Willie. "Do you have two together?"

Grandpa Simple saw Uncle Maynard Simple walking a cute little poodle.

"I got it for my wife," Uncle Maynard said proudly.

"You made a smart trade," replied Grandpa Simple.

When Cousin Elmer Simple's girlfriend came down with a cold, he brought her a gift-wrapped package of cough drops.

"You could have at least brought flowers," complained the girl.

"I heard you were sick," said Cousin Elmer, "not that you'd died."

MR. SIMPLE: I wonder what causes so many divorces in this country.
MRS. SIMPLE: Marriage.

MR. SIMPLE: You're a hard woman to please.
MRS. SIMPLE: No, I'm not. After all, I married
you, didn't I?

Why does Susie Simple love homework.
**It gives her something to do while she
watches TV.**

When Uncle Maynard Simple got married, he
told his bride that marriage and a career don't
mix.
And he hasn't worked a day since.

"My wife is an angel," said Grandpa Simple.

"You're lucky," replied Great Uncle Abner Simple. "Mine's still alive."

SUSIE SIMPLE: I can't go to school today, Mommy.

MRS. SIMPLE: Why can't you?

SUSIE SIMPLE: I feel sick.

MRS. SIMPLE: Where do you feel sick?

SUSIE SIMPLE: In school.

Great Uncle Abner Simple went to the grocery store every day and bought a case of dog food. Finally, the curious store manager said, "You must have a lot of dogs."

"Don't have any," said Great Uncle Abner. "This is for my wife. It's all she'll eat."

"Mister, that's terrible!" exclaimed the shocked store manager. "If you keep feeding this to her, you'll kill her."

"I don't have any choice," replied Great Uncle Abner Simple. "Like I said, this is all she'll eat."

So, for the next several weeks, Great Uncle Abner continued to buy a case of dog food every day. But then one day he came into the store and bought a sirloin steak.

"What, no dog food today?" asked the store manager.

"Nope," replied Great Uncle Abner Simple. "My wife died yesterday."

"I told you that would happen," said the manager, shaking his head.

"It wasn't the dog food that killed her," said Great Uncle Abner. "She was chasing a car and got run over by a truck."

Why did Grandpa Simple have to go to the hospital after he put a muffler around his neck?

Someone started the car.

GRANDPA SIMPLE: When I was a young man, I shot a lion in my pajamas.

SUSIE SIMPLE: Gee, how did the lion get your pajamas on?

Cousin Elmer Simple was so stupid that he stayed up all night studying for his blood test the next morning.

GREAT AUNT SALLY SIMPLE: I'd like a double banana split with chocolate, vanilla, and strawberry ice cream. I also want lots of nuts and whipped cream.

WAITER: Do you want a cherry on top?

GREAT AUNT SALLY SIMPLE: No, I'm on a diet.

At a family gathering, Mr. Simple was bragging about the race horse he had just bought.

"That horse is as smart as I am," he said proudly.

"You'd better shut up," said Mrs. Simple. "Someday you might want to sell that horse."

Great Uncle Abner Simple always ate with his fingers. He said, "That's because if food isn't clean enough to pick up, then it isn't clean enough to eat."

Cousin Cindy Simple was taking a shower when the doorbell rang. She got out of the shower and yelled, "Who's there?"

"Blind man," was the response.

So Cousin Cindy opened the door. In walked a man with a long package. "Do you want me to hang these Venetian blinds for you?" he asked.

Aunt Edna Simple was awakened from a sound sleep when the phone rang at 4:00 A.M. "Is this Joe's Pizza Parlor?" asked the person on the other end of the line.

"No," replied Aunt Edna.

"I must have gotten the wrong number," said the voice. "Sorry I woke you."

"Oh, that's okay," said Aunt Edna Simple. "I had to get up anyway. The phone was ringing."

BOYFRIEND: If you don't marry me, I'll hang myself from that tree in your front yard.

COUSIN CINDY SIMPLE: Please don't do that. You know my parents don't want you hanging around here.

COUSIN CINDY SIMPLE: I think trial marriages are dangerous.

AUNT EDNA SIMPLE: Why's that, dear?

COUSIN CINDY SIMPLE: Because they can lead to the real thing.

44

Susie Simple went to a fortune-teller and said, "Both Bobby and Jimmy are in love with me. Which one will be the lucky guy?"

The fortune-teller looked into her crystal ball and said, "Bobby will marry you. Jimmy will be the lucky one."

GRANDMA SIMPLE: Poor little Willie lost his dog, Leroy.

GRANDPA SIMPLE: He should put an ad in the paper.

GRANDMA SIMPLE: Don't be silly! Leroy can't read.

Great Uncle Abner Simple had three pairs of glasses: one for reading, one for distances, and one for looking for the other two.

TEACHER: Do you have any questions, class?

COUSIN IDA SIMPLE: I do.

TEACHER: Yes, Ida?

COUSIN IDA SIMPLE: Where do the words go when you rub them off the blackboard?

Farmer Jake Simple was so ugly that whenever he shaved he sneaked up on the mirror.

Great Uncle Abner Simple invented a great lotion for balding men. It shrinks their heads so that what hair they have looks like more.

TEACHER: Willie, tell the class where the English Channel is.

WILLIE SIMPLE: Gee, I don't know. We don't get it on our TV set.

Cousin Elmer Simple took his girlfriend to the opera and was jealous when she said, "Doesn't that handsome tenor sing beautifully?"

"I would, too, if I had a voice like that!" snapped Cousin Elmer.

Why did Uncle Maynard Simple marry a midget?

So she could look up to him.

"Boy, it's hot out today," complained Willie Simple.

"Why don't you take some cold tablets?" replied Susie Simple.

Boss: Didn't you get my letter saying you're fired?

Cousin Elmer Simple: Sure, I got it, but the envelope said, "Return to sender after five days," so here I am.

Aunt Edna Simple: Doctor, I think strawberries are growing in my ears.

Doctor Sigmund Simple: Now, how could that have happened?

Aunt Edna Simple: I don't know. I planted peas.

SUSIE SIMPLE: Mommy, are the new people across the street poor?

MRS. SIMPLE: No, why you do ask?

SUSIE SIMPLE: They sure were upset when their baby swallowed a dime.

WILLIE SIMPLE: Can I go outside and play?

MRS. SIMPLE: With those holes in your jeans?

WILLIE SIMPLE: No, with the kids next door.

GREAT AUNT IRMA SIMPLE: What are those things you've got there?

FARMER JAKE SIMPLE: Cattails. Haven't you ever seen cattails before?

GREAT AUNT IRMA SIMPLE: Nope, not without the rest of the cat.

COUSIN ELMER SIMPLE: Have you ever seen a man-eating fish?
COUSIN CINDY SIMPLE: Yes.
COUSIN ELMER SIMPLE: Where?
COUSIN CINDY SIMPLE: In a restaurant, of course.

Great Aunt Irma Simple, who was interested in ecology, explained that she had been married so many times because she believed in recycling her husbands.

GRANDMA SIMPLE: How much sugar should I put on your cereal, dear?
SUSIE SIMPLE: Too much, please.

GREAT UNCLE ABNER SIMPLE: How did you find the weather when you went to the mountains?

COUSIN ELMER SIMPLE: Easy. I just went outside, and it was there.

DOCTOR SIGMUND SIMPLE: Have you ever had an accident?

FARMER JAKE SIMPLE: Nope.

DOCTOR SIGMUND SIMPLE: Never, in your whole life?

FARMER JAKE SIMPLE: Well, last summer my horse threw me.

DOCTOR SIGMUND SIMPLE: And you don't call that an accident?

FARMER JAKE SIMPLE: Nope. Horse did it on purpose.

TEACHER: Willie, if I had ten apples and sixteen children, how would I divide them equally?

WILLIE SIMPLE: I don't know about you, but I'd make applesauce.

51

TEACHER: It's nine o'clock. You should have been here an hour ago.
SUSIE SIMPLE: Why? What happened then?

Cousin Martha Simple was such a hypochondriac that she took every medicine imaginable.
Whenever she sneezed, sick people around her were cured.

Doctor Sigmund Simple told Grandpa Simple that glasses would change his view of the world.
Now he has three glasses of beer a day.

MR. SIMPLE: If you were in the jungle and a rhinoceros charged you, what would you do?
SUSIE SIMPLE: Pay him.

TELEVISION REPAIRMAN: The only thing wrong with your TV set is a short circuit in the cord.
GRANDMA SIMPLE: For goodness' sake, make it longer, then.

CUSTOMER: Waitress, will my breakfast be long?
CINDY SIMPLE: The sausage probably will be, but the pancakes will be round.

UNCLE MAYNARD SIMPLE: Doc, that lotion you
gave me makes my arm smart.
DOCTOR SIGMUND SIMPLE: Then I suggest you
put some on your head.

Susie Simple lost her wallet, and her brother
Willie found it.
Now she's looking for Willie.

MRS. SIMPLE: If you truly loved me, you'd buy
me a mink.
MR. SIMPLE: Okay, but you've got to promise to
keep its cage clean.

Why did wealthy Aunt Agatha Simple buy a new refrigerator?

The old one was empty.

Great Uncle Abner Simple was so fat that his wife had to let out the shower curtain.

MRS. SIMPLE: Are you afraid of the dark, Susie?
SUSIE SIMPLE: No, not when you leave the light on.

Doctor Sigmund Simple felt sorry for his poor patients. When they couldn't afford an operation, he touched up their X rays.

GREAT UNCLE ABNER SIMPLE: Do you sing professionally?
AUNT AGATHA SIMPLE: I only sing to kill time.
GREAT UNCLE ABNER SIMPLE: That's quite a weapon you have there.

Cousin Elmer Simple liked to go to the beach to watch the pretty girls. One day Uncle Abner Simple went with him. After a while, Uncle Abner said, "You certainly like bathing beauties, don't you?"

"Gee, I don't know," replied Cousin Elmer. "I never bathed any."

Susie Simple was being chased by Billy, who lived next door. When Mr. Simple saw what was happening, he grabbed Billy and yelled, "Why are you chasing Susie?"

"Because she hit me," said Billy.

"Is that true, Susie?"

"Yes," said Susie.

Releasing Billy, Mr. Simple said, "Why did you hit him?"

"So he'd chase me," she replied.

MRS. SIMPLE: Why are you crying?
SUSIE SIMPLE: Willie broke my doll.
MRS. SIMPLE: How'd he break it?
SUSIE SIMPLE: I hit him over the head with it.

MRS. SIMPLE: Why are you running so fast?
WILLIE SIMPLE: I'm trying to stop a fight.
MRS. SIMPLE: Who's fighting?
WILLIE SIMPLE: Elmer and me.

Cousin Elmer Simple was bragging about his promotion at the sanitation department. "Now," he said proudly, "I drive the garbage truck, and I have two helpers under me."

"That's not much," said Cousin Bert Simple. "I'm a foreman at the bottling factory, and I have twelve men under me."

Uncle Maynard Simple, bored with their bragging, said, "I've got a more responsible job than both of you put together."

"Oh, yeah," said Cousin Elmer and Cousin Bert together. "What's your big job?"

"I have over twenty thousand people under me," replied Uncle Maynard Simple, proudly.

Cousin Elmer and Cousin Bert were impressed until Uncle Maynard added, "I cut the grass at the cemetery."

Aunt Agatha Simple complained to her rich husband, Archibald Simple, "You must fire that new chauffeur. He nearly killed me three times today."

Uncle Archibald Simple thought for a minute, and then he said, "Ah, let's give him one more chance, my dear."

Cousin Elmer Simple gave his girlfriend a fur coat, a new sports car, and an expensive diamond ring.

But when he proposed to her, she turned him down, saying, "I wouldn't marry a man who throws money around as foolishly as you do."

Why didn't Grandma Simple put ice in her lemonade?

She forgot the recipe.

Mr. Simple and Uncle Maynard Simple were walking down the street together when they saw Uncle Maynard's wife going into a movie theater with another man.

"Aren't you going to go after them?" asked Mr. Simple.

"Why should I?" replied Uncle Maynard. "I've already seen the movie."

Mr and Mrs. Simple spent the evening at home trying to do a jigsaw puzzle.

They finally gave up after a couple of hours, because they couldn't get the two pieces to fit together.

Cousin Elmer Simple got a job at a restaurant and got mad when people called him a waiter. "The customers do the waiting here," he complained.

Willie Simple put a slug in the fortune-telling scale. A card came out of the slot and read: "You are handsome, brave, and honest."

It got his weight wrong, too.

Why was Aunt Irma Simple pleased when the fortune-teller called her a half-wit?

She only had to pay half price.

Why did Grandma Simple back out of the bus?

Because she heard one man ask another, "Are you going to grab that old lady's seat when she gets off?"

TEACHER: What would you like me to talk about today, class?

WILLIE SIMPLE: About five minutes, and then let us go home.

WILLIE SIMPLE: Our dog, Leroy, is like a member of the family.
COUSIN CINDY SIMPLE: Yeah, I see the resemblance.

Susie Simple's teacher was trying to think of a nice way to tell her her poems couldn't be used in the school paper.

"Did you make these up yourself, Susie?" she asked.

"Yes," replied Susie. "Aren't I a good poet?"

"You wrote these all by yourself?"

"Out of my head," said Susie.

"That's what I thought," said the teacher.

When Susie Simple was late for the first three days of school, her teacher asked her why.

"Well," said Susie, "every time I get to the corner down the street, I see the sign that says, 'SCHOOL, GO SLOW.'"

GRANDPA SIMPLE: I hope I'm sick.

DOCTOR SIGMUND SIMPLE: Why would you hope a thing like that?

GRANDPA SIMPLE: I'd hate to feel this way if I'm well.

WILLIE SIMPLE: Go wash your face, Susie. I can see what you had for breakfast this morning.

SUSIE SIMPLE: I bet you can't.

WILLIE SIMPLE: Sure I can. You had eggs.

SUSIE SIMPLE: Ha, ha. No, I didn't. That was yesterday!

GREAT UNCLE ABNER SIMPLE: I hear Cousin Mort Simple came down with a high fever yesterday. How's his temperature today?

GRANDPA SIMPLE: I don't know. He died last night.

GRANDMA SIMPLE: How much are the eggs?
FARMER JAKE SIMPLE: The regular eggs are one dollar a dozen. The cracked ones are fifty cents a dozen.
GRANDMA SIMPLE: Okay, crack me a dozen.

Farmer Jake Simple visited the city for the first time. When he got to Main Street, he stopped because the light was red. After it had changed to WALK, he scratched his head in confusion. But he finally got out of his truck and walked across the street.

SUSIE SIMPLE: Girls are a lot smarter than boys.
WILLIE SIMPLE: Yeah? I never heard that.
SUSIE SIMPLE: See what I mean?

TEACHER: Susie, name two pronouns.
SUSIE SIMPLE: Who, me?
TEACHER: Very good.

MRS. SIMPLE: How'd you get that black eye?
WILLIE SIMPLE: I was hit by peaches.
MRS. SIMPLE: Peaches gave you a black eye?
WILLIE SIMPLE: They were in a can.

COUSIN ELMER SIMPLE: Does your dog, Leroy, have a license?
SUSIE SIMPLE: Of course not, he's not old enough to drive.

GRANDPA SIMPLE: Give me a cup of coffee without cream, please.
WAITER: I'm sorry, sir. We're out of cream, but I can give you a cup of coffee without milk.

MR. SIMPLE: I have great news. We have enough money to go to Europe this summer.
MRS. SIMPLE: That's wonderful. When can we leave?
MR. SIMPLE: Soon as we save enough money to get back.

GRANDPA SIMPLE: I just can't remember anything these days.
DOCTOR SIGMUND SIMPLE: How long have you been this way?
GRANDPA SIMPLE: What way?

MR. SIMPLE: Who was that on the phone?

SUSIE SIMPLE: Just someone who said it was long distance from London. I said it sure was.

GRANDMA SIMPLE: I've really been sick since I ate a dozen clams yesterday.

DOCTOR SIGMUND SIMPLE: Were they fresh?

GRANDMA SIMPLE: I don't know.

DOCTOR SIGMUND SIMPLE: How did they look when you opened the shells?

GRANDMA SIMPLE: What shells?

Farmer Jake Simple went into a hardware store carrying an empty birdseed box. Angrily, he said, "I want my money back. This seed isn't any good."

"What's wrong with it?" asked the store clerk.

"I planted it three months ago, and not a single bird has come up."

TEACHER: If you found a five-dollar bill in one pocket of your pants and a ten-dollar bill in another pocket, what would you have?
WILLIE SIMPLE: Somebody else's pants.

TEACHER: If you had five sticks of gum and Willie asked for one, how many would you have left?
COUSIN ELMER SIMPLE: Five.

SUSIE SIMPLE: What are the holes in this piece of wood?
WILLIE SIMPLE: They're knotholes.
SUSIE SIMPLE: If they're not holes, what are they, then?

68

TEACHER: What month has twenty-eight days?
COUSIN BERT SIMPLE: They all do.

The phone rang at four o'clock in the morning and woke Grandma Simple from a sound sleep.

"I'm your next door neighbor," said an angry man, "and your dog is making such a racket that I can't sleep." With that, he hung up before Grandma Simple could say anything.

The next morning at four o'clock, Grandma Simple went to the phone and called her neighbor.

When the sleepy neighbor answered, Grandma Simple said, "I'm just calling to tell you I don't own a dog."

MR. SIMPLE: I got another note from your teacher saying you're failing history. What's the problem?
SUSIE SIMPLE: It's not my fault. The teacher always asks about things that happened before I was even born.

"Has anyone seen my baseball mitt?" yelled Willie Simple.

"Did you look in the car?" asked Mrs. Simple.

"Yeah," said Willie, "but it's not there."

"Did you try the glove compartment?" asked Mr. Simple.

SUSIE SIMPLE: Daddy, you're still growing, aren't you?

MR. SIMPLE: No, of course not. Why do you say that?

SUSIE SIMPLE: Because I can see the top of your head coming through your hair.

WILLIE SIMPLE: Wow! That's a great stuffed tiger you have. Where'd you get it?

UNCLE MAYNARD SIMPLE: In India, when I was on a hunting trip with my grandpa.

WILLIE SIMPLE: What's it stuffed with?

UNCLE MAYNARD SIMPLE: My grandpa.

Grandma Simple went to Doctor Sigmund Simple's office and said, "I hurt everywhere. My head hurts. My feet are sore, I've got a stomachache, and my back hurts, too."

Doctor Sigmund Simple said, "Sit here, and let your legs hang over the edge of the table."

She did, and then the doctor picked up a little hammer and tapped Grandma Simple's knees to check her reflexes. "How do you feel now?" he asked.

"Terrible!" moaned Grandma Simple. "Now my knees hurt, too."

Cousin Elmer Simple went to the farm to visit Farmer Jake Simple. They had been in the barn for about ten minutes when Cousin Elmer said, "You sure have a lot of flies here."

"Yep, we do," replied Farmer Jake.

Cousin Elmer swatted at one and said, "Don't you ever shoo them?"

"Nope," said Farmer Jake. "We just let 'em go barefoot."

GRANDMA SIMPLE: What's that picture you're drawing?

SUSIE SIMPLE: It's a picture of heaven.

GRANDMA SIMPLE: Why, Susie, no one knows what heaven looks like.

SUSIE SIMPLE: They will when I'm done, Grandma.

COUSIN BERT SIMPLE: What has twenty-eight legs, two hundred sharp teeth, twenty eyes, and is yellow and green?

FARMER JAKE SIMPLE: I don't rightly know.

COUSIN BERT SIMPLE: Neither do I, but there's one outside in your pig pen.

Cousin Elmer Simple and Willie Simple took their girlfriends to the county fair. After they had walked around for a while, Cousin Elmer and his girlfriend decided to try the tunnel of love.

When they came out, they were drenched. "What happened?" asked Willie. "Did the boat leak?"

Cousin Elmer looked at him with a surprised expression, and said, "What boat?"

Cousin Elmer Simple and Willie Simple were watching a video movie about horse racing. As a race was about to begin, Willie said, "I'll bet you a dollar that number seven wins the race."

"You've got a deal," said Cousin Elmer, shaking Willie's hand.

Number seven did win, but when Cousin Elmer started to pay his debt, Willie said, "You don't have to pay me. I watched this movie yesterday."

"So did I," said Cousin Elmer, "and I didn't think the horse could win two days in a row."

GRANDPA SIMPLE: I sure am homesick.
GRANDMA SIMPLE: But you are home.
GRANDPA SIMPLE: And I'm sick of it.

Uncle Archibald Simple was teaching Aunt Agatha Simple how to drive. She was doing fine until she came to a red light. She stopped, but when it changed to green, she didn't move. The light changed several times, but she stayed where she was.

Finally, Uncle Archibald couldn't stand it, and he said, "What are you waiting for?"

Aunt Agatha replied, "For a nice shade of blue."

Susie Simple was very proud when she put her shoes on all by herself. She ran to show her mother.

Mrs. Simple said, "Very good, Susie, but you have them on the wrong feet."

A confused look came on Susie's face, and she said, "But, Mommy, they're the only feet I have."

Cousin Elmer Simple went to a department store to buy some fancy soap for his mother's birthday present.

"Do you want it scented?" asked the salesperson.

"No," replied Cousin Elmer, "I'll take it with me."

Aunt Edna Simple always tells people that Cousin Elmer is slow because he was born a week after his birthday.

TEACHER: Do you know how deep the Hudson River is?

WILLIE SIMPLE: Not very deep.

TEACHER: Why do you say that?

WILLIE SIMPLE: Well, I once saw a duck on it, and the water only came up to his stomach.

FARMER JAKE SIMPLE: What are you doing up in
my tree?
COUSIN ELMER SIMPLE: One of your apples fell
down, and I'm just trying to put it back.

TEACHER: Susie, if I lay one egg on my desk,
another on my chair, and another on the
floor, how many will there be?
SUSIE SIMPLE: There won't be any.
TEACHER: Oh! And why not?
SUSIE SIMPLE: Because you can't lay eggs.

WILLIE SIMPLE: Can you write with your eyes
closed?
MR. SIMPLE: Probably. What do you want me to
write?
WILLIE SIMPLE: Your name on my report card.

Mrs. Simple learned that old Mr. Smith down the street was sick. "Willie," she said, "why don't you go ask how old Mr. Smith is."

"Okay," said Willie, and he hurried out the door.

A little later Willie came back to the house and said, "Mr. Smith told me to tell you it's none of your business how old he is."

Uncle Maynard Simple felt terrible when he ran over Grandma Simple's cat and killed it. He went up to her house, and after telling her what had happened, he said, "I would like to replace it."

Grandma Simple looked at him skeptically and then asked, "Can you catch mice?"

Mrs. Simple: Have you changed the water in your fishbowl?
Susie Simple: No. They haven't drunk it all yet.

FARMER JAKE SIMPLE: Would you like to take this chicken home to eat?

COUSIN ELMER SIMPLE: Boy, I sure would! But what does it eat?

AUNT AGATHA SIMPLE: Waiter, what is this bug doing on my ice-cream sundae?

WAITER: Madam, I believe it's skiing downhill.

COUSIN CINDY SIMPLE: What time is it, Susie?

SUSIE SIMPLE: I don't know, but I know it's not six yet.

COUSIN CINDY SIMPLE: Oh, how do you know that?

SUSIE SIMPLE: Well, because Mommy said I have to be home at six. I'm not home yet, so it can't be six.

Cousin Martha Simple called Doctor Sigmund Simple and said, "Cousin Willie's dog, Leroy, just bit my leg, and I'm in a lot of pain."

"Did you put anything on it?" asked Doctor Sigmund Simple.

"I didn't have to," replied Cousin Martha. "Leroy liked it plain."

SUSIE SIMPLE: What time is it, Grandpa?

GRANDPA SIMPLE: It's half past two.

SUSIE SIMPLE: Not again!

GRANDPA SIMPLE: What's wrong?

SUSIE SIMPLE: You're the fifth person I've asked for the time today, and you've all told me something different.

COUSIN ELMER SIMPLE: I don't think it's fair for you to give me a zero on this test.

TEACHER: Neither do I, but it's the lowest grade I can give.

DOCTOR SIGMUND SIMPLE: Why are you always hopping around on one foot?

COUSIN BERT SIMPLE: To keep the ghosts away.

DOCTOR SIGMUND SIMPLE: There aren't any ghosts around here.

COUSIN BERT SIMPLE: See, it works.

Why does Farmer Jake Simple put suntan lotion on his chickens?

Because he likes dark meat.

Why is Leroy, the Simple family dog, always hot in the summer?

Because he wears a coat and pants.

Aunt Agatha Simple and Uncle Archibald Simple were driving through the countryside toward Boston when they realized they were lost. They happened to see a relative, Farmer Jake Simple, walking along the road.

Uncle Archibald stopped the car and called out, "Hi there, Jake!"

"Hello," replied Farmer Jake.

"Can you tell us how to get to Boston?" asked Aunt Agatha.

"Nope, reckon I can't," said Farmer Jake.

"Well, do you know where the nearest gas station is?" asked Uncle Archibald.

"Nope," replied Farmer Jake.

"You certainly don't know very much," said an exasperated Aunt Agatha.

"That may be," said Farmer Jake, "but at least I'm not lost."

Susie Simple was sitting on the porch steps when a woman came up to her and asked, "Is your mother at home?"

"Yes," replied Susie.

The woman knocked several times, but there was no answer. She finally turned back to Susie and said, "I thought you told me your mother is at home."

"She is," said Susie, "but I don't live here."

WAITER: Do you want your coffee black, sir?
UNCLE MAYNARD SIMPLE: What other colors do you have?

MRS. SIMPLE: Why did you swallow the dollar I gave you?
SUSIE SIMPLE: You told me it was my lunch money.

DOCTOR SIGMUND SIMPLE: How is Great Aunt Sally Simple doing with her weight reduction diet?
GREAT UNCLE ABNER SIMPLE: Very well. She disappeared three days ago.

TEACHER: Do you know what a comet is, Willie?

WILLIE SIMPLE: A comet is a star with a tail on it.

TEACHER: Can you name one?

WILLIE SIMPLE: Lassie.

COUSIN ELMER SIMPLE: Is it true that a tiger won't attack you if you carry a big stick?

GRANDPA SIMPLE: It all depends on how fast you carry it.

AUNT EDNA SIMPLE: Do you know how to prevent infection caused by biting insects?

FARMER JAKE SIMPLE: Reckon I do.

AUNT EDNA SIMPLE: How?

FARMER JAKE SIMPLE: Don't bite any.

Susie Simple went to the zoo with Grandpa Simple. After they had been to the lion's cage, she asked, "Grandpa, will a lion hurt you if you run away from it?"

"Well," replied Grandpa Simple thoughtfully, "it all depends on how fast you run."

WILLIE SIMPLE: I can lift an elephant with one hand.
SUSIE SIMPLE: No you can't.
WILLIE SIMPLE: Find me an elephant with one hand, and I'll prove it to you.

AUNT EDNA SIMPLE: I don't know if we should swim here. I heard there are alligators.
UNCLE MAYNARD SIMPLE: There's nothing to worry about. The crocodiles will scare them away.

Why did Farmer Jake Simple make his chickens swim in hot water?

So they'd lay hard-boiled eggs.

Uncle Maynard Simple went out to the country to visit Farmer Jake Simple. When he got there, he was astonished when he saw Farmer Jake playing chess with a large pig.

"This has to be the smartest pig in the world!" exclaimed Uncle Maynard.

"Don't know about that," replied Farmer Jake Simple. "I've beaten him two out of three games today."

SUSIE SIMPLE: I want to buy a pillowcase for my grandpa.
STORE CLERK: What size do you want?
SUSIE SIMPLE: I'm not sure, but Grandpa wears a size seven hat.

Why did Cousin Bert Simple lose his job as a weatherman?

The weather didn't agree with him.

UNCLE MAYNARD SIMPLE: Cindy, what would you do if a man-eating lion chased you?
COUSIN CINDY SIMPLE: Nothing.
UNCLE MAYNARD SIMPLE: Nothing! Why?
COUSIN CINDY SIMPLE: Because I'm a girl.

TEACHER: I'm afraid you didn't pass the history test. Your answers weren't very good.
WILLIE SIMPLE: Well, I didn't think much of your questions.

Great Aunt Sally Simple and Great Uncle Abner Simple were happy to be among the passengers on the world's first totally automated flight.

They weren't so happy, though, when they heard a recorded voice say, "Ladies and gentlemen, welcome aboard the world's first fully automated flight. We want to assure you that nothing can go wrong . . . go wrong . . . go wrong . . ."

UNCLE ARCHIBALD SIMPLE: Waiter, there's a fly in my pea soup.
WAITER: There's nothing to worry about, sir. I'll take it back and exchange it for a pea.

At a family dinner, Cousin Elmer Simple had been annoying everyone by reaching across the table. Finally, his mother said, "Stop reaching for your food. You have a tongue, so use it."

A confused expression came to Cousin Elmer's face. "Why, Mom? My arm's longer."

Cousin Bert Simple, who was talking to Grandpa Simple, said, "When I grow up, I want to have millions of dollars and a huge mansion with no showers or bathtubs."

Grandpa Simple scratched his head and asked, "Why no showers or bathtubs?"

"I want to be filthy rich," was Cousin Bert's reply.

GREAT AUNT EDNA SIMPLE: How'd you get that big bump on your nose?

GREAT UNCLE ABNER SIMPLE: I tried to smell a brose in the garden.

GREAT AUNT EDNA SIMPLE: There isn't a B in rose.

GREAT UNCLE ABNER SIMPLE: There was in the one I smelled.

WILLIE SIMPLE: Why are you looking over your new glasses instead of through them?

GREAT AUNT IRMA SIMPLE: I don't want to wear them out.

COUSIN BERT SIMPLE: Something is terribly wrong with me, Doctor. I keep thinking I'm a butterfly.

DOCTOR SIGMUND SIMPLE: Oh, dear! How long has this been going on?

COUSIN BERT SIMPLE: Since I was a caterpillar.

Susie Simple was bragging about her brother to Cousin Cindy Simple. She said, "Willie has been playing the trumpet for five years."

Cousin Cindy Simple shook her head and said, "Boy, I bet his lips are sore."

Have YOU heard any good ones lately? If you have and would like to see them in print, turn them into Simple Family jokes and send them to:

Adam Bryan
P.O. Box 646
Woodstock, NY 12498

Remember, no compensation or credit can be given, and only those "Simple" enough will be included.

ABOUT THE AUTHOR

Adam Bryan is a pseudonym for the author of several books for young readers, published primarily by Avon-Camelot. The father of four sons, Mark, Wyatt, Bryan, and Adam, all of whom have contributed to this book, he lives near Woodstock, New York, where he is at work on a family history and another Simple Family collection.

THEY'RE MORE THAN

FUNNY...

THEY'RE LAUGH-OUT-LOUD

HYSTERICAL!